# LEARNING TO SAY MY NAME

## NIKITTA DEDE ADJIRAKOR

Published by Akashic Books
©2023 Nikitta Dede Adjirakor
ISBN: 978-1-63614-123-7

Akashic Books
Brooklyn, New York
Instagram, Twitter, Facebook:
@AkashicBooks
E-mail: info@akashicbooks.com
Website: www.akashicbooks.com

African Poetry Book Fund
*Prairie Schooner*
University of Nebraska
110 Andrews Hall
Lincoln, Nebraska 68588

# TABLE OF CONTENTS

# PREFACE

*by Victoria Adukwei Bulley*

"And now, what do I do with my scars?"

Such is the question posed by Ghanaian poet Nikitta Adjirakor's speaker of "Under the Rainbow," one of fourteen poems gathered here. Perhaps it is helpful to begin the chapbook they comprise, tenderly titled *Learning to Say My Name*, by thinking about the nature of scars. Scars are those parts of our bodies that tell our history through what once were wounds; they are sometimes subtle, known only to ourselves at, other times they are raised ostentatiously above the skin in spite of us. Yet what better way to understand the body—the poems that form *this* body of work—than through markers of human experience so multivalent that they can symbolize both harm and healing?

It is in exactly this way, then, that Adjirakor's poetry navigates themes of gender, motherhood, lineage, and grief. In one of the most striking poems, "Becoming a Mother," her speaker takes to imagining herself as pregnant—not with a baby but as the parent to benign growths that have been residing within her:

> Lately I've been nourishing these tumors
> inside me, thinking of myself as a mother,
> running my hands over my rounded body
> and looking for a heartbeat that isn't there.

The poem tells of the speaker's heartbreak but it does so at a slant. Instead of directly lamenting the absence of a child within the womb, or the presence of tumors in the first place, Adjirakor takes the poem in a different and more startling direction by illustrating the unexpected ways that even grief itself can be creative. This kind of reckoning with pain looks like resignation at first but is, at a closer glance, indicative of a speaker with courageous emotional integrity. Here, "honest" also means the possibility of "finding consolation / in a wound."

Elsewhere in the chapbook, it is family that takes center stage—with appearances from the speaker's mother, and shadowy presences of older male and paternal figures whose abuse harms those who most need their care. "Family is a father you've never seen sober," writes Adjirakor. Family, too, is made or unmade through naming, particularly within the Ga customary traditions that Adjirakor refers to across several poems. In the titular poem, "Learning to Say My Name," names are linkages—a means of signifying relation. But what happens when family breaks down, when an inheritance is less than a blessing? Asking these questions, Adjirakor interrogates the work performed by the name "Dede" when the father-daughter connection it implies has been shattered: "If a name is untethered from a father," she asks, "does it live?" There is richness in the word "untethered"—it contains as much freedom as it does precarity—while the question "does it live?" suggests just how much is at stake. Even where living is a likelihood, a given name continues to haunt like a ghost: "just because a thing is alive," writes Adjirakor, "does not mean it is whole." ("Home Is Not Here in This Body")

Indeed, life is a delicate process. Both in its coming forth and its continuance, its staying; the newborn that breathes beyond its eighth day, the daughter who looks at a photograph of her grandmother, sees "her gap tooth in my mother's mouth / my mother's in mine" (Annual Family Portraits). Life repeats and replicates just as much as it bears its fragilities. Faith falters as the physical form fails. And yet, even as I am wary of the imperative to write toward happy endings, it must be noted that the poems of *Learning to Say My Name*, heavy as they are, do not sing of surrender. Nor are they poems of making peace. Perhaps they might best be read as poems that know *ongoingness*, a tightrope-walking between the uneasy paradoxes of loss and love, of life and death, past and future.

It is striking how the words *body* and *love* are inescapable throughout, each one occurring as many times as the other. It's as though Adjirakor is compelling us to remember something too easy to forget: love as the body that does its best, the body as a vessel for love, stumbling as it may be, still whole enough to ask, "love me again, love me *despite*." ("Annual Family Portraits")

## IN THE HOSPITAL

I cannot tell you when we begin to fold into each other, my mother and I, even though there is a door separating us. While she is held together by middle-aged women, shaking and whimpering in her kaba, told to grieve properly by swallowing herself, I am fastened to a bed by a doctor who touches me like I am the lake he wants to drown in. I choke on my whispered, *I've never been touched like that before* as the doctor scoffs because I am sin he has uncovered and the nurse mutters sorry like a calculated prayer. Says *I am a university girl* as he spreads my knees. Says *I must like doing it with the boys* as his hands plunge between my thighs. Says *he is the act before a husband* as the nurse strokes my forehead. I want to tape my moans into his mouth and show him surrender but these moans are familiar, a library of the woman who raised me and these moans are in my head like a trophy searching for wounds to breathe in.

## MY SAVIOR, SHE BLEEDS
## OR: 1 IN 10 WOMEN HAVE ENDOMETRIOSIS

I've spent years dying without death
and now I worship
the unnamed woman in the Bible
who bled for 12 years.

*I asked how you would rate your pain.*

On a scale of 1 to 10,
the wounds have voices.

*What do they say?*

That death too is a journey
and like my body, elastic
enough to harbor everything.

*Which number do they choose between 1 and 10?*

They say my body is a sentence
for many verbs.
I am folding
and I am folded.
Its place is not with me.

*Which number?*

An open wound I arrange myself around.
I iron my tongue and stack

the diagnosis
neatly.

*If you'll just give me a number.*

12, like my savior clogged
with blood, glowing
as she finds her savior.

## ON THE OCCASION OF AN OUTDOORING WHEN YOU TEACH A CHILD TO STAY

Eight days after we died, Mother taught me to spell death.
She is fluent in loss versified in her bones.

I round my mouth and let God stay next to death.
I am cursed to stumble toward birth.

How many paths must I dare seek to unravel myself
from the threads of my mother's cloth?

There's rain trying to wash me away or is it alcohol?
Before I drown, I hold out my finger and let corn wine teach me truth.

How God and death wrestle in my mouth.
This moment, my only inheritance.

This moment, this eighth day, my resurrection.
I weep as I hear God sieve my prayers through my mother's

cloth. An archive of life that hears death.
The patterns humming over unassembled cribs.

My mother hems her grief. I touch the seams
and feel the splinters of life at my fingertips.

We pretend the water that fills her eyes has not
burrowed into our lungs to drown us.

Before I drown, I hold out my finger
and let raindrops teach me existence.

There's something about the eighth day. Name becomes meaning
and you return to that place that calls you home and you answer.

And when you name, you grasp reliably at two things:
what is named and what births.

My mother carries belonging with her.
She is tethered to the living and the dead.

She is now. I am a possibility that will not be answered.
These hands are eager to consume her image that sits on both our bodies.

On the occasion of my resurrection when all are gathered,
I am wrapped in my mother's cloth.

We sit next to our bodies
while I inherit songs hemmed into fraying cloths.

This is how we love.
inheriting eyes that fixate on spaces between the unsaid.

## UNDER THE RAINBOW

I am learning that when they say a rainbow baby,
they mean our names have lost their music
which is to say that death is present
and I am a memorial and a prayer.

They mean our feet wear hope
and how dare you linger on the grief
that threatens to spill with each step.

I have buried myself before.
Dig deep into the bikini cut and find pieces of joy next to my kidney.
By that I mean I have taken over from the surgeon,
sewing pieces of myself into places they cannot be seen.

This is why my mother loves in loneliness.
Everyone tries to love in the present tense–here and now.
Meanwhile my mother is a house with rooms built out of possibility.

Loneliness has taught her to love what has been and what could be.
Today, I need these hands empty to pull her into the present.
Love me so I remember how to wear my body again.

And now, what do I do with my scars?
Dig deep into the bikini cut and tuck in my grief.
Smear shea butter onto it to smoothen their words
when they say, *at least you can try again.*

How about you let me sink into my mother's thighs and let these scars breathe.
How about you let me fold myself into these scars and question this wound.

When they say a rainbow baby, they mean my body is a bed of resurrection and everything stays with me.

## LINEAGE

My mother tongue fights behind stapled teeth
that only loosen for other languages.

Sometimes, it inches through my gap tooth punctuating
each sentence with *oh* and *eh*,

a discordant symphony that announces
its foreignness.

The instructor asks, "What is your native language?"

Where native means mother tongue,
which means my father's tongue,
which was removed when his mouth contoured
into a home for a different self.

The instructor acts surprised.
*Which language did you speak first?*

My grandfather acts surprised.
*Which language are you speaking now?*

When my grandfather says *naakpɛɛ*, it means his surprise happens in Ga,
which literally means his mouth is stitched together,
which suggests we do not speak,
which suggests we cannot speak,
which is to say trauma is buried in his tongue into mine.

I build a home out of loss, and split

myself to sew his embarrassment into me. In Ga,
I thirst, for his shame–*ehie egbo*
Literally, his face is dead,
because death is the lineage I have inherited.

The instructor asks again: "I mean, what was your local language before
you were colonized?"

I've been running my tongue enough times over my gap tooth to know
the ache I feel as it widens is my grandfather emerging from my mouth.

I know it is the only space left to pack and unpack who we are not.

## LEARNING TO SAY MY NAME

I have planted my mother in my mouth
so that when I say *I love you,*
she can curl around the words,
but my language is not enough for her
and my *I love you* is dimming the glow out of this sun.

I grasp unreliably at my mother's lineage,
that sits on both our bodies.
She says I am claimed by my father and his father
who announced my belonging as her water broke
My father is dead
I lose what slippery connection I had

I hyphenate my name with hers,
create a dash to form belonging,
till we are two parts of a whole and
when I say *I love you,*
I am tethered to her forever

But my name, Dede, is an unnaming
shy of the warmth she needs
Dede, the first daughter asks, *the first daughter of whom?*
If a name is untethered from a father, does it live?

## GLASS BEADS

The girls are half-naked, floating through the streets as they arrive into
   womanhood.

You watch them with envy because you still have to close your eyes
when people kiss on the television,
and Daddy won't let you join the initiation, *because we are Christians.*

The beads rounding their waists are heavier than yours
and you wonder if Daddy can rip them off like he did yours last night.

## HOME IS NOT HERE IN THIS BODY

I too want to remember how to wear my body again. In this house, everything remains unfinished and we mistake resignation for patience. I was named after a father's hope, a future appointment that leaves me untethered in the present. Perhaps this is why I fold into myself, close my fists and wait for the world's permission to be(come). When your name is a stranger, faith is what wears your feet through each door that arrives at nothingness. I ask myself, what is faith if not the emptiness I choke on while washing it down with possibility? Yet, mother tells me faith is all we have and when I filter the world through her gaze, I see her again. Longing for a lover's promise. Waiting for a daughter's survival. In my body everything remains unfinished and I mistake emptiness for peace. I am at war with myself. Home is not here in this body. On another trip to the emergency room, I ask the doctor to find my selves and pass them on to me. These hands are free to grasp them like a desperate prayer. When your name is a stranger, you learn that just because a thing is alive does not mean it is whole. By that I mean I have forgotten how to wear a body that is whole. I mean home is not here in this body. I mean even as I meet myself with violence, speak tenderness into me.

## SONGS OF FAITH

When her baby died, they put her in a room with women singing
praise songs to their Gods of miracles.
Faith holds her mouth open, forcing her to swallow the women's songs.
What God asks her to dance into the grave and gives faith a shovel?

She tries hard to remember the face of someone
who only glanced at the world.
If she dies possessed by longing, could she drag the baby back into her body?
She is a graveyard swallowing graves of pity.

Some ghosts were never people
and when we grab the arm of the night to draw us a map
to where they wait, the night already forgot what they smelled like,
and we have no name to call them by.

The pictures of smiling toothless babies remind her
that absence is a kind of death for those who are present.
And who will greet her when she returns home
into a self that forgot how to be finished?

## ANNUAL FAMILY PORTRAITS

My grandmother's face hangs on the wall in my mother's house,
her gap tooth in my mother's mouth,

my mother's in mine. Or is it my grandmother's?
When my mother taps me at dawn kissing God into my mouth,

she calls it a celebration. Who better to give me life
and have you ever seen a man before the naming?

Some days I am not a girl.
I am an open womb, an open wound

and no one wants to believe I am going mad.
No one believes. I am going mad.

The dentist asks to close my gap tooth
because it serves no purpose.

Have you tried to write a poem about mouths
that were not at war with the world?

Each time I speak, my tongue is coated in loss.
My mother asks for grandchildren and

my body stays silent, homing
~~people~~ beings that only come to die.

After I hold grief between my palms, take it and love it,
I tell my grandmother we can chase silence together.

Its cadences eager to linger in rooms with no open windows.
We find it in my mouth I cannot answer to

sitting rock heavy and weighting my jaw
till I realize the gap tooth is a filter

for a world searching to drop its pain in someone's stomach.
When we find loneliness so thick, obese enough

that it shapes like a human and holds our hands,
we let it lead in prayer.

Grief is the ritual through which I say
love me again, love me *despite.*

## LIVING ANCESTORS

Maybe these are not all my stories to tell
but I need you to understand that trauma
is another way of saying we have died
many deaths.

# WOMAN WAITS FOR ULTRASOUND TO TURN COLORFUL

Hope does not want these legs
growing thinner descending to the earth.
But these legs tap music into hope,
each rhythm creating holy ground
and slitting the throat of the night
to reveal the texture of a love beyond survival.
My parents loved me in grayscale,
each grain planting new names on their tongues
till I reached out and touched God in their mouths.
I apologize when I talk about my body,
whisper *defective* before quoting poetry
about mothers hemorrhaging into fertile lands
and planting stories synonymous to decay.
Like the moment my mother began as a mother
and the doctor neatly tucked her insides as blood trickled down her legs,
she hid parts of herself around the globe
tied together by her scars slowly decaying
till they turned into dust and a quivering madness.
A most spectacular madness.
As these legs grow thinner toward the earth,
they snake around searching for my mother's selves
to teach me to love in grayscale, to love these grains
that only use me to search for places to bloom.

## BECOMING A MOTHER

Lately I've been nourishing these tumors
inside me, thinking of myself as a mother,
running my hands over my rounded body
and looking for a heartbeat that isn't there.

Perhaps there is something to be said
about madness, about finding consolation
in a swollen body that is an empty home
simply because it is a sign of possibility.

I've been trying to find language
that does not swallow my consolation
and no matter how they say it,
*sorry*, *kpo kpo*, there is something

disrespectful about how they choke
on my solace, as if finding consolation
in a wound that has made a home
out of me is not too an act of love.

## PRAISE STRUCK

Praise your Lord God of hope
and praise your pastor who says your blessings doubly abound
which means double double,
because everything happens here in twos.
Our lives need permission to exist and then to confirm
how to wear the world.
Praise your Lord God of miracles
and praise your pastor who reminds you
your father was a twin, and ends
by saying, *afi be nɛ nɛ,*
which means next year by this time
which sounds like

• a prophecy—you will soon be pregnant
• a declaration—white is the color of celebration
• an irony—white is your grief in the present

Family is a father you've never seen sober
and men whose tears have never touched your fingers.
Family is the loneliness you pray into your chest and the resilience
you wear during each burial in your mind like your mother did
before you for the children that didn't stay. Praise wears
your fingers and scratches your throat sore. What is
a little discomfort for the promise of a body that lives
and stretches beyond itself. You want to know joy that lives
and floods and rounds and pulses. Joy that wears white
without a calendar. Joy that harbors more joy. So, you fall
on your knees and let God fill your mouth and when you begin
to feel joy lingering in your bones, reach out with soft hands and take it.

## ACKNOWLEDGMENTS

The poem "Learning to Say My Name" appeared in a different form in the nonfiction piece "Bodies of Loss" published by *SAND Journal.*